Ivo Peters' CLASSIC STEAM

Ivo Peters'
CLASSIC STEAM

Mac Hawkins

David & Charles

A DAVID & CHARLES BOOK
Copyright © Mac Hawkins 1996
Photographs copyright © Julian Peters

A catalogue record for this book is available from the British Library.

ISBN 0-7153-0490-9

Designed and typeset by Character Graphics, Taunton
and printed in England by Butler & Tanner Ltd, Frome
for David & Charles
Brunel House Newton Abbot Devon

HALF TITLE PAGE
Lyncombe Vale, Bath
A superb worm's eye view of S&D Class 7F No 53807, still fitted with its large diameter
boiler, climbing hard through Lyncombe Vale with the 12.35 down freight from Bath.
The rear of the train is yet to emerge from the 440yd Devonshire Tunnel, where the
banking engine's crew are undoubtedly experiencing unpleasant conditions, not aided by
the train engine's exhaust which is still hanging inside the bore. *27 March 1954.*

FRONTISPIECE
Bristol Barrow Road shed
The ex-Midland shed always offered an interesting variety of motive power as subjects for
Ivo Peters' camera lens. Using the Barrow Road bridge as a frame and a half-full gasometer
as a backdrop, he captures Stanier 'Black Five' 4-6-0 No 44851, Jubilee class No 45662
Kempenfelt and 2-6-0 'Horwich Crab' No 42890 on shed to produce a memorable image of
steam traction in its heyday. *15 June 1958.*

CONTENTS

ACKNOWLEDGEMENTS

My sincere thanks go to Julian Peters, who kindly consented to my doing this book. He also helped me delve into his father's extensive collection to select photographs for inclusion in this volume; an onerous task indeed. When struggling to choose prints, he kept me on the straight and narrow by reminding me that 'classic' was the byword! In addition, Julian spent many hours looking through his father's notebooks for caption material to enable me to include many previously unpublished prints from the Ivo Peters' Collection.

It would be remiss of me not to mention and thank Lydia Peters for her generous hospitality on many visits to her home and for kindly checking the manuscript to ensure no split infinitives had crept in accidentally!

Thanks must go to Derek Mercer whose printing skills have been well utilised in interpreting Ivo Peters' photographs so beautifully; and also to Dave Rankin and Gerard Hill, who proofread and edited the manuscript in double-quick time. In addition, they helped me considerably with technical and geographical matters where I was uncertain.

Mark Curnock of Character Graphics has again shown great tolerance and exercised considerable patience with my exacting demands, so special thanks go to him for designing this superb volume.

Finally I would like to pay a special tribute to my wife, Jenny, for reading the first drafts as they came hot off the printer and for the endless patience shown in helping me with the selection of photographs when indecision ruled!

INTRODUCTION

Ivo Peters, whose name became synonymous with the Somerset & Dorset line, was without doubt one of the finest railway photographers to have captured on film the last few decades of steam traction in Britain and Ireland. As an aesthete and perfectionist, his *penchant* was to photograph steam trains as they passed through spectacular countryside and he took infinite care to frame the 'perfect shot'; this approach epitomised his exacting style.

Although his first love was the Somerset & Dorset, the tortuous $71\frac{1}{2}$-mile line between Bath and Bournemouth, the less obviously photogenic urban or industrial scene was not forgotten: throughout the 1950s and until the mid-1960s he travelled the length and breadth of the country to visit many smaller and private lines. If it were not for his straying off the beaten track, so to speak, unlike many other photographers of the period, these historical scenes might otherwise have gone unrecorded. In the 1960s the National Coal Board, breweries, docks, shipyards, power stations, ironstone mines, quarries and foundries still operated dozens of steam locomotives of infinite variety. Ivo Peters was allowed access to a number of these widely-scattered industrial environments to photograph steam engines at work. A few pictures, mainly taken at since-closed collieries, are included in this volume as a small sample from the vast collection he assembled.

The narrow gauge lines of Wales, the Isle of Man and Ireland (notably the delightful Tralee & Dingle Light Railway) were not overlooked and these too became subjects for his camera lens, spanning many years post-war. In April 1965 he made the first of several trips to Westmorland and Yorkshire to record the dying days of steam on the West Coast main line and the Settle & Carlisle route. His final visit to the North-West was made in the spring of 1967 – a little over a year before BR steam finally passed into the annals of history. With the demise of his beloved S&D line as a through route in 1962 and its inexorable end in sight (which finally came on 6 March 1966), Ivo Peters became increasingly attracted to the Southern Region to record the last years of steam, which ended in July 1967. He concentrated on the Salisbury–Exeter and Bournemouth–Weymouth routes, and their associated branch lines, before the Beeching Axe took a swipe at them.

Travelling from his home in Bath, Ivo was often accompanied by his great friend Norman Lockett, also a keen railway photographer, so that they might share the great pleasure to be derived from these trips and they would sometimes meet up with other notable exponents of the camera such as Derek Cross and Dick Riley. He was also able to share his love of trains with another close friend: the Reverend Teddy Boston was an enthusiastic steam fan and Ivo made several visits to the ecclesiastic's private railway in the grounds of Cadeby Rectory, which he copiously recorded on film. We are fortunate that Ivo Peters has left a legacy of so many enduring images with his photographs (and movie film) which others are now able to enjoy.

In the early 1980s Ivo Peters became seriously ill, eventually becoming bed-ridden and no longer able to pursue his skills as a photographer. It was shortly before he died in the summer of 1989 that he suggested the author should have access to his photographic collection for publishing purposes and with the co-operation of his son, Julian, this volume featuring some of Ivo Peters' best work has been made possible.

Mac Hawkins
1996

Bath Green Park

Class 2P 4-4-0 No 40700 sets off from Bath Green Park on a lovely sunny autumn afternoon with the 13.10 down stopping train for Templecombe.

The station opened on 4 August 1869 as 'Bath Queen Square', the terminus of the Midland Railway's extension from Mangotsfield. The station welcomed a newcomer on 20 July 1874, when the Somerset & Dorset's Bath extension was opened, joining the Midland's line at Bath Junction a half-mile due west of the terminus. An agreement allowed joint running on the short section into the station, which became the S&D's northern terminus. Although four lines ran into the station, it had only two platforms; the two middle roads were used for running round and for storage. After railway nationalisation the station was renamed 'Bath Green Park'. *2 November 1957.*

Bath shed (1)

A wonderful study of a variety of locomotives inside the Somerset & Dorset's wooden-trussed engine shed, which was built alongside the Midland's but at a slightly lower level.

Among those in residence are large-boilered S&D Class 7F 2-8-0 No 13807,

still carrying its old number and with LMS lettering on its tender. Another member of the class, No 53810, has the smaller boiler of 4ft 9^1/$_8$in diameter and carries its new BR number, but both are from the batch built in 1925. In the background is Class 4F 0-6-0 No 44235. The shed code at this date was 22C. *25 February 1950.*

Bath shed (2)

Despite the obvious fire risk, the timber-trussed shed is seen in similar condition thirteen years later – although the motive power has changed. Double-chimneyed BR Class 4 4-6-0 No 75071, simmering quietly inside the gloomy interior, is partially lit by piercing rays of sunlight adding to the dramatic effect of this exquisite picture.

The locomotive was transferred from Exmouth Junction (72A) to Bath (71G) in June 1956 and worked the line until closure in March 1966. However, by the time this photograph was taken, it was in temporary residence at Bath MPD (since 23.2.58, coded 82F), having been assigned to Templecombe (82G) shed in November 1962. *4 May 1963.*

Bath departure (1)

Having taken over the 09.15 from Birmingham, one of Bath's Class 2P 4-4-0s, No 40700, and BR Class 4 2-6-0 No 76028 from Eastleigh (71A), set off with little fuss from Green Park with the Saturdays-only train for Bournemouth. They pass the stone-built Midland engine shed, entrance to which was gained via a 60ft turntable. In the background two other locomotives are standing astride the bridge over the River Avon, on the far side of which the station's overall roof can be seen through the smoke haze. *3 September 1955.*

Bath departure (2)

Smoke and steam galore: in contrast to the other departure shot, BR Class 4 4-6-0 No 75072 sends a towering plume of black smoke shooting skywards as it leaves Bath Green Park with the 16.37 down local; however, it is actually being momentarily outrun by 2-6-4T No 80146 coming away from the turntable in front of the Midland shed in determined style!

On the left Britannia Pacific No 70034 *Thomas Hardy,* a class rarely seen at Bath, stands wreathed in smoke on the coaling plant road and awaits another duty on a northbound train; it was based at 5A Crewe North MPD. The axle loading of the Britannias prevented them from working over the S&D line. *1 May 1965.*

Devonshire Bank, Bath
With its billowing exhaust almost reaching to the heavens, S&D 7F 2-8-0 No 53800 puts in a mighty effort as it lifts the 12.35 goods to Evercreech Junction out of Bath up the steep 1:50 gradient towards the Maple Grove pedestrian bridge where Ivo Peters is standing, just beyond which it will enter the narrow bore of the $1/4$-mile Devonshire Tunnel.

No 53800 is being ably assisted at the rear by a Class 4F 0-6-0, which will see the train through Devonshire Tunnel and into Lyncombe Vale; it will only drop off the rear once the summit has been reached at the entrance to Combe Down Tunnel, 30 chains beyond. *28 April 1951.*

Lyncombe Vale, Bath (1)

A heavily wooded valley set less than a mile from the city centre, this was a favourite location for Ivo Peters to capture trains as they passed between the two narrow bore tunnels on the stiff climb out of Bath.

A breath of fresh air for the footplate crew of Class 7F No 53810 as it emerges from the stifling conditions in Devonshire Tunnel into Lyncombe Vale with the 08.55 down goods from Bath to Evercreech Junction. It still has a little climbing at 1:50 to do through the vale before plunging into the much longer, but equally restricted, bore of Combe Down Tunnel just over a quarter of a mile away.

Lyncombe Vale, Bath (2)
Caught in the glorious sunshine of a crisp spring morning, Class 7F 2-8-0 No 53806, with the 11.20 down freight from Bath, works hard on the 1:50 gradient as it crosses over Watery Bottom Viaduct in Lyncombe Vale and climbs towards Combe Down Tunnel. In the background the banker can be seen emerging from Devonshire Tunnel. *19 March 1955.*

Combe Down Tunnel, Bath (1)

With scenes like this, it is not difficult to understand why Ivo Peters' first love was the Somerset & Dorset and he chose many superb vantage points along the 71$\frac{1}{2}$-mile line in order to secure the best aspect of trains as they worked hard on this tortuous route between Bath and Bournemouth.

The crews of Class 2P 4-4-0 No 40569 and Standard Class 5 4-6-0 No 73047 on the 'Pines Express', the Somerset & Dorset's premier train, can take advantage of the fresh air as they emerge into Lyncombe Vale and the sparkling sunshine of a bright spring day, having endured the fuliginous atmosphere in Combe Down Tunnel.
6 April 1957.

Combe Down Tunnel, Bath (2)

This fabulous shot of Class 2P 4-4-0 No 40696 assisting S&D 7F 2-8-0 No 53804 with the 07.35 (SO) Nottingham–Bournemouth is a true classic: at the end of the hard climb out of Bath, the train is seen approaching the northern portal of Combe Down Tunnel and is about to plunge into the 1,829yd-long bore. The permanent way hut and associated water trough, together with the small viaduct beyond, over which the locomotives are passing, all add to this delightful scene.

To ensure this vista was not obstructed by branches and foliage, Ivo Peters occasionally undertook some judicious pruning with the use of a heavily weighted length of whipcord to haul the offending branch close enough to lop off! Today this area constitutes part of a scenic footpath through the vale and remains reasonably clear. *29 June 1957.*

Horsecombe Vale

At the southern end of Combe Down Tunnel, trains emerged into Horsecombe Vale and more open countryside; they then crossed the impressive structure of the eight-arch Tucking Mill Viaduct, 96yd long and some 63ft above the valley it spanned.

On a misty Friday afternoon, Maunsell Class U1 2-6-0 No 31906, assisted by Class 2P 4-4-0 No 40563, crosses the viaduct and climbs the 1:55 gradient towards Combe Down Tunnel with the 11.40 from Bournemouth.

Both the U and U1 classes of Southern locomotives were being assessed for possible use over the S&D line and trials were carried out over a two-week period, working specially-composed trains of eight and 12 coaches. In the event, they were not deemed suitable for the steeply-graded route. *12 March 1954.*

Tucking Mill Viaduct *(left)*

This superb shot not only offers a striking view of this elegant structure set in the wooded surroundings of Horsecombe Vale, but also shows its proximity to Combe Down Tunnel in the background.

On a glorious spring day, the down 'Pines Express', hauled by Class 2P No 40564 and Stanier Class 5 4-6-0 No 45440, is seen crossing the viaduct. Just over the roof of the first coach is Midford's down distant upper-quadrant signal, of Southern Railway origin: the post is made from old rail sections bolted together – a far cry from the more elegant lattice structures built by the LSWR. *21 April 1951.*

Park Bank, Midford *(above)*

After crossing Tucking Mill Viaduct, the line curved south-west through a short rock cutting to pass the grounds of Midford Castle (quaintly built to form the ace of clubs) and Midford's goods yard, from where this picture was taken. BR Class 4 2-6-0 No 76015 and Class 9F 2-10-0 No 92220 *Evening Star,* working the 09.55 Bath–Bournemouth, sweep downhill past the castle grounds towards the 66yd tunnel known as the 'Long Arch Bridge' on the approach to Midford station.

No 92220 had just been specially transferred to Bath to work the last 'Pines Express' on 8 September 1962, a date which would also mark the end of all through trains on the Somerset & Dorset line. *1 September 1962.*

Midford valley (1)
Midford valley rendezvous: with the up outer home signals set firmly in the on position, the now-preserved S&D Class 7F 2-8-0 No 53809 waits with an up freight for the single-line section into Bath, whilst 7F No 53806, approaching with the 17.00 down freight for Evercreech Junction, swings into view as it heads southwards.

This location, a few hundred yards south of Midford station and the viaduct, was a firm favourite of Ivo Peters, who made countless visits to this valley. He was usually sure of being able to record such scenes as this at the point where trains would pass, as one of them waited for the single-line section to clear. Some of the wonderful North Somerset countryside through which the line ran is well illustrated in this fine shot.
11 June 1957.

Midford valley (2)

Seen sweeping through the reverse curves at Lower Twinhoe are Templecombe-based Class 2P 4-4-0 No 40569 and West Country class Pacific No 34045 *Ottery St Mary* (from 71B Bournemouth shed) with the 09.25 (SO) Bournemouth–Manchester. Sadly, the 2P had only a couple of months left in service.

The S&D followed closely the course of the Radstock arm of the old Somersetshire Coal Canal (later a tramway), which was laid down during the latter half of the 18th century and used to convey coal from the mines around Radstock to the canal basin at Midford. The grades on this section were relatively slight and the line undulated gently, following a rather erratic serpentine-like course as it closely hugged the hillside. This provided ample opportunity to capture some memorable photographic images, like this one. *12 August 1961.*

Wellow valley

Equally picturesque, the Wellow valley also proved an ideal location for the photographer: here the down 'Pines Express' snakes through the beautiful valley and heads towards Wellow, about a mile to the south. In charge of the train is the S&D's omnipresent Class 2P No 40569 and BR Class 5 4-6-0 No 73049, which was also a regular performer on the line.

From January 1957 the latter spent no fewer than five years on the S&D and, apart from a period between April 1960 and July 1962 allocated to Shrewsbury, it worked on the route until it was eventually transferred to 81F Oxford in September 1964, where it was finally taken out of service in March 1965. No 40569 was withdrawn in November 1961 and reduced to scrap at Crewe Works a month later. *11 May 1957.*

Wellow (1)

An evocative shot of Stanier 'Black Five' 4-6-0 No 44888 and West Country class 4-6-2 No 34043 *Combe Martin,* with the down 'Pines' relief, heading south-west from Wellow, a small village set in rural isolation a few miles south of Bath and served by the S&D.

Ivo Peters' daughter, Diana, stands at a field gate to wave to two of her friends, drivers Bert Brewer with the LMS Class 5 and Donald Beale on the SR Pacific, as the train hurries past. The tower of St Julian's church in Wellow can just be spotted over the rear of the train.
27 September 1958.

Wellow (2)
Standing in a field just south of Wellow village, Ivo Peters manages to create an idyllic leafy vista to frame BR Class 4 2-6-0 No 76057 as it runs towards Bath with the 13.10 up local from Bournemouth.

The Class 4 locomotive was allocated to 70F Bournemouth shed in November 1959 and regularly worked S&D diagrams up until closure of the line in March 1966. It was to soldier on for another few months, eventually being withdrawn in October and after a short time spent in storage at Eastleigh MPD, was sent for scrap to Cashmore's, Newport, where it was cut up in July 1967.
18 September 1965.

Norton Hill, Midsomer Norton

The assault of the testing 7½-mile climb of the Mendips began in earnest at Radstock, the town at the centre of the coal mining industry in Somerset.

Here Class 7F 2-8-0 No 53807, with the 11.00 down freight for Evercreech Junction, slogs up the 1:50 gradient unassisted towards Midsomer Norton station. It is about to pass the sidings at the entrance to Norton Hill Colliery, from which much mineral traffic was generated.

Heavy freight trains were normally banked from Radstock to the summit at Masbury, 811ft above sea level. The banker would then return 'wrong line' to Binegar (having picked up a tablet on the way through) and back to Radstock to await another duty.

No 53807 was the last of the eleven of the class to remain in traffic before its withdrawal in October 1964; it was reduced to scrap at Cashmore's, Newport, between January and April 1965. *27 September 1963.*

Midsomer Norton (1)
The Southern Region, on assuming responsibility for the motive power (all of which was on loan from the London Midland Region), conducted trials in March 1951 with Bulleid light Pacifics to assess their suitability for the route. As a result, four were allocated to Bath shed (81G) to assist with the heavy summer traffic; they were Nos 34040 *Crewkerne,* 34041 *Wilton,* 34042 *Dorchester* and 34043 *Combe Martin.*

  A striking shot of one of these Pacifics, No 34040 *Crewkerne,* makes a splendid sight in this snowy winter scene, as it prepares to stop at Midsomer Norton with the 09.55 down semi-fast from Bath to Bournemouth. *30 January 1954.*

Midsomer Norton (2)
With a healthy-looking exhaust emitting from its chimney, Class 7F 2-8-0 No 53802 pulls away from Midsomer Norton with a down freight from Radstock and tackles the 1:53 gradient in spirited fashion on the climb to Chilcompton Tunnel about a mile to the south. The attractive 16-lever box on the station's up platform (seen in the background) was usually adorned with hanging baskets in the summer months and provided a riot of colour, along with the well-tended flower beds on the station platforms, for passengers and staff to enjoy.

Midsomer Norton was a frequent winner in the annual 'best kept station' competition: between 1953 and 1960 it enjoyed an unbeaten run. This event followed a tradition instituted by the Joint Committee in 1913 and was an eagerly fought contest; it typified the pride shown by S&D staff in 'their' railway.
16 April 1955.

Chilcompton Tunnel (1)
A mile south of Midsomer Norton station, this short twin-bore tunnel, 66yd long and built on a curve, was another favourite haunt of Ivo Peters. He took many shots of trains here as they tackled the arduous southbound climb over the Mendips; there were still four miles to go until the summit at Masbury.

Captioning this picture 'foreign coal and an east wind', he caught Class 2P 4-4-0 No 40568 and Standard Class 5 4-6-0 No 73050 bursting from the tunnel in a volcanic eruption of smoke and steam as they blasted up the 1:53 gradient with the down 'Pines Express'.
25 February 1956.

Chilcompton Tunnel (2)

If looks could deceive . . . BR Class 9F No 92220 *Evening Star,* in a very grubby state, bursts from the tunnel with a roar as it pounds up the gradient towards Chilcompton Bank. Despite the amount of smoke belching from the exhaust, the load was light: only three coaches constituting the 13.10 down local from Bath!

  Having been transferred to the line the previous year for three months, primarily to work the last 'Pines', then allocated to 81F Oxford in October 1962, the locomotive returned to the S&D the following year and spent from August until October working local services: a far cry from its design capabilities. With several locomotives away under repair, Bath became short of motive power, which necessitated the loan of replacements; Class 5s had been requested, but two 9Fs were sent instead. *7 September 1963.*

Chilcompton Tunnel (3)
A final glimpse of this photogenic location. This time the amount of effort is justified as Class 5 4-6-0 No 73051 emerges from the tunnel in a swirling halo of smoke and is seen making an excellent climb of the Mendips with an eight-coach Whit-Monday excursion from Bath to Bournemouth.

No 73051 was a stalwart of the S&D line and spent all of its working life on it. When brand-new, it was one of three to be allocated to Bath in May 1954, along with Nos 73050 and 73052. It was withdrawn in August 1965, a couple of months after this photograph was taken, and stored at Bath MPD until October; it was finally sent to Cashmore's, Newport, and broken up in November. *7 June 1965.*

Chilcompton station

After leaving the tunnel at Chilcompton, the line steepened to 1:50 for nearly a half-mile and curved through a short rock cutting towards the station. On a cold and frosty morning with a mackerel sky adding to the dramatic lighting effect, Class 7F 2-8-0 No 53801 – one of the 1914 series of locomotives built for the S&D – comes storming through Chilcompton with the 08.55 down goods from Bath to Evercreech Junction.

Chilcompton was used as a watering hole for banking engines on their return to Radstock – the water tower can be seen on the right.

The 13-lever signal box controlled the small yard, which once handled coal brought by road from New Rock Colliery nearby.
23 November 1957.

Emborough – Burnt House Bridge

Having just passed under Burnt House Bridge (No 57) and the 700ft contour line, but still climbing hard with about 2½ miles to go to the summit, Class 2P 4-4-0 No 40697 and BR Class 5 No 73019 haul a Bristol–Bournemouth Whit-Sunday excursion towards the twin-arch bridge (No 58) at Moorewood on which Ivo Peters is standing. His friend Norman Lockett, seen on the embankment, has already taken a photograph of the train. On the down side of the line, it will shortly pass Moorewood Colliery's sidings, which closed in 1930. A few chains further on the up side is the 19-lever signal box, controlling the section and entrance to Emborough Quarry's sidings. *21 May 1961.*

Masbury – Oakhill Road Bridge (1)

The struggle is nearly over: large-boilered Class 7F 2-8-0 No 53806 with the 16.05 down coal train from Midsomer Norton, assisted in the rear by Class 3F 0-6-0T No 47496, approaches Bridge 69 carrying the B3135, as it climbs the last few yards on the 1:73 gradient to Masbury Summit. Once the banker has seen the train over the summit, it will return wrong-road to Binegar; a procedure made possible with a bank engine staff having been picked up from the tablet-exchange apparatus as it passed through. *25 May 1953.*

Masbury – Oakhill Road Bridge (2) *(left)*
A very unusual picture taken from almost the same spot shows Class 7F 2-8-0 No 53805, having just breasted the summit with an up goods, as it shoots from under the road bridge and heads towards Binegar, about a mile northwards.

The footplate crew cheerily acknowledge Ivo Peters standing on the bridge: perhaps a measure of the high esteem in which S&D staff held him. In the 1950s and 1960s Ivo became a familiar figure to most of the footplate crews as he took pictures up and down the line. It was his custom to circulate any recently-taken photographs in order that staff might be able to choose prints in which they featured.
30 May 1950.

Masbury Summit *(right)*
A sight soon to disappear: the 'Pines Express' breasting the summit at Masbury, 811ft above sea level. With just under five weeks to go to the re-routing of the 'Pines' and the ending of all other through trains over the Somerset & Dorset, BR Class 4 4-6-0 No 75009 and BR Class 9F 2-10-0 No 92001 make a powerful combination as they drag the 09.45 Bournemouth–Manchester over the crest of the Mendips.

If asked which was his favourite S&D location, Ivo Peters, without equivocation, said: "Masbury!". He spent many happy hours watching trains struggling to conquer the line's pinnacle and in the process took countless photographs and shot yards of 16mm movie colour film. He also enjoyed the fruits the lineside offered in summer – wild strawberries. *4 August 1962.*

Masbury Halt

Captioned 'a very rare sight' in his album, this stirring picture shows the up 'Pines' passing through Masbury Halt on a stormy day. The train engine is Stanier 'Black Five' 4-6-0 No 44830 and the pilot large-boilered S&D 7F 2-8-0 No 53806. The usual pilot – a 2P 4-4-0 – had been commandeered to work a down train when a Bulleid Pacific had failed at Evercreech Junction.

It was very unusual at this juncture in the line's history for the 7Fs to be used on passenger workings; however, it became increasingly common during the 1950s and early 1960s to see these sturdy workhorses being employed on such diagrams. Although there was reluctance to use the 2-8-0s at first, they more than proved their worth on such duties, particularly when motive power was in short supply on a busy summer Saturday. *3 November 1951.*

Shepton Mallet

Snap! Having followed it from Bath by car with his son Julian, Ivo Peters takes a picture of Class 7F 2-8-0 No 53803, which is having its tender replenished and is about to leave Shepton Mallet with the 12.35 down freight to Evercreech Junction. Class 7F 2-8-0 No 53810, with black smoke blasting from its exhaust, suddenly appears from behind the stone-built goods shed and thunders past with an up freight for Bath. The crew of No 53810 were taking advantage of the brief downhill stretch through the station to the halfway mark over the 27-arch 317yd Charlton Viaduct before tackling the final 3½-mile climb to Masbury Summit, nearly all of which was at a gruelling 1:50. In the background is the attractive S&D-designed 26-lever signal box sited in the middle of the down platform, behind which is the large tank supplying the water cranes at each end of the station. *21 April 1956.*

Cannard's Grave

Cannard's Grave Summit was reached in a cutting straddled by several bridges. This location often provided spectacular (if somewhat noisy!) photographic opportunities for Ivo Peters, since northbound trains were inevitably to be seen working at their hardest on the continuous 2½-mile section at 1:50, part of the 4½-mile climb from Evercreech Junction to Shepton Mallet.

Here Class 2P No 40700 and BR Class 5 No 73051 toil up the final half-mile stretch towards Shepton Mallet with the 10.35 Bournemouth–Manchester and pass under Bridges 90 and 89. *23 August 1958.*

Evercreech Junction

Organised by the Locomotive Club of Great Britain, a special train ran over the S&D system between Broadstone and Bath and was hauled by S&D Class 7F 2-8-0 No 53808, whilst for the run over the branch from Evercreech Junction to Burnham-on-Sea, ex-GWR Collett 0-6-0 No 3210 was used.

Here No 53808 makes a good start away from Evercreech Junction for Bath.

There are plenty of enthusiasts hanging out of the carriage doors and windows to get the full benefit of the 7F's healthy exhaust bark as it pulls away from the up platform. Railway buffs are still able to appreciate the same sounds today, since No 53808, preserved as S&D No 88 by the Somerset & Dorset Railway Trust, runs on the West Somerset Railway. *30 September 1962.*

Cole Viaduct
On a tranquil summer's evening, cattle munch contentedly in the lush meadow in the lee of Cole Viaduct and are quite undisturbed by BR Class 5 4-6-0 No 73068 as it rushes northwards with the 15.40 up mail from Bournemouth. A connection with the evening mail train from Bristol to the North had to be made at Mangotsfield, on the Midland main line, so the 15.40 had priority over all other traffic on the S&D.

Cole was the meeting place of the Dorset Central and the Somerset Central, which joined here in 1862 to form the Somerset & Dorset Railway. The viaduct, which spanned a farm track and the River Brue just north of the station, was demolished on 12 September 1984. *31 August 1965.*

Shepton Montague

The stretch between Cole and Wincanton was moderately graded, which meant some fast running could be achieved in either direction. The elegant twin-arch bridge (No 127), carrying a minor road over the line which passed through a shallow cutting, was another favourite location of Ivo Peters.

BR Class 9F 2-10-0 No 92210 speeds under Rock Cutting Bridge with the 10-coach 07.40 (SO) Bradford–Bournemouth, as driver Bert Brewer and passed fireman Peter Smith lean out from the cab grinning broadly. They had spotted Ivo standing at the lineside and rewarded him with an emission of black smoke from the locomotive's chimney, and are obviously pleased with their enterprising salute! *21 July 1962.*

West Pennard (left)

The 22-mile branch line from Evercreech Junction to Highbridge ran dead straight across the Somerset Levels for much of its length. This view taken from the A361 road bridge at the east end of West Pennard station illustrates the point well and is full of interesting detail (including a rather fine 'carver' chair in the goods shed, picked out by a shaft of sunlight). It shows the line extending into the distance, straight as a die for four miles towards Glastonbury.

This country station served a rural community and seen here is ex-GWR 0-6-0 No 3206 with the 14.20 Highbridge–Templecombe local waiting to re-start from West Pennard on a blustery autumn day. With the easy running on the branch mostly behind it, a little more effort will be required to climb to the summit of Pylle Bank, some 3³/4 miles away; however, the gradients would be no more severe than 1:86 and generally not nearly so steep. *3 November 1962.*

Catcott Crossing (above)

A perfect mirrored image of Class 4F 0-6-0 No 44560 in charge of 'The Southern Wanderer', a special organised by the Southern Counties Touring Society. This ran from London Victoria to Bournemouth and over the S&D to Evercreech Junction, thence up the branch to Highbridge and back. The train is seen passing Catcott Crossing in the middle of the Somerset Levels on its return to Templecombe. Earlier in the day engines had been changed at Templecombe and No 44560 took over. The 4F was once shedded at there, but on this occasion had been borrowed from Gloucester MPD; it was withdrawn two months later and scrapped in December.

The branch to Highbridge was originally the main line of the S&D, which had its Works there. The S&D crossed the GW main line and continued for 1¹/2 miles to Burnham-on-Sea, terminating at a pier beyond the station. At one time passengers could transfer to a steamer for the crossing to South Wales. *28 March 1965.*

LONDON & SOUTH WESTERN LINES

Bournemouth, Hampshire (1)

The picturesque tree-lined cutting west of Bournemouth Central provides an attractive setting to capture Merchant Navy class 4-6-2 No 35028 *Clan Line* as it swings through with the 09.25 Weymouth–Waterloo towards the station; but first it will have to pass the motive power depot on the east side of the bridge on which Ivo Peters is standing.

After withdrawal in July 1967, *Clan Line* was purchased by the Merchant Navy Locomotive Preservation Society and initially based at Bulmers, Hereford. Today it is normally based at Southall and is in main line running condition, following a further rebuild in 1994/5. *20 June 1964.*

Bournemouth, Hampshire (2)

A classic view of Bournemouth Central station, from the road bridge at the eastern end, shows two classes of Bulleid Pacifics, one rebuilt and the other in original condition with air-smoothed casing. Merchant Navy 4-6-2 No 35022 *Holland-America Line* pulls out of the station with a three-coach train from Weymouth, whilst Battle of Britain light Pacific No 34076 *41 Squadron* stands on a centre road awaiting a path.

Whilst No 34076 was scrapped at Cashmore's, Newport, in November 1966, No 35022 was saved and is preserved on the Swanage Railway. *10 October 1965.*

Hayling Island branch, Hampshire

This 4^1/$_2$-mile branch line, built by the London, Brighton & South Coast Railway and opened in 1867, had a severe weight restriction imposed by a wooden swing bridge over the entrance to Langstone Harbour. This necessitated the use the diminutive LBSCR 0-6-0 'Terrier' tanks designed by William Stroudley in 1872 and rebuilt by D. Earle-Marsh in 1911 as the A1X class.

A fabulous shot of No 32661, seemingly dwarfed by its two-coach train, having crossed Langstone Bridge on its way to Hayling Island on a crisp autumn morning. Of interest is the spark arrester on its chimney, a precaution against setting fire to the wooden structure it had just traversed! Although No 32661 was scrapped at Eastleigh Works in August 1963, eight of the class have been privately preserved – a testament to their popularity. The Havant–Hayling Island branch closed on 4 November 1963. *6 October 1959.*

Wimborne, Dorset

Shortly after passing Broadstone Junction and the connection with the Somerset & Dorset line, Drummond M7 0-4-4T No 30048 crosses the River Stour with the 14.25 Bournemouth–Brockenhurst local and draws near to Wimborne.

This was on the former LSWR Dorchester–Waterloo main line via Hamworthy and Ringwood, which had lost most of its importance when a causeway was built over Holes Bay linking Hamworthy and Poole in 1893, after which through trains were generally routed via Bournemouth. The line finally closed to passenger traffic on 4 May 1964. *5 August 1963.*

Poole Harbour, Dorset *(left)*
Boats and trains, but no planes: the sight of a steam engine working in the tight confines of a dockside or harbour, with all its potential hazards and clutter, often produces images which are incomparable. Here ex-LSWR Class B4 0-4-0T No 30093, from 71B Bournemouth shed, negotiates the quayside with a short goods train. What looks to be an ex-Royal Navy Fairmile 'B'-type ML, now civilianised and named *Matapan,* rests at its moorings and comes under the scrutiny of a member of the public and two smartly-attired shunters standing further back. Just visible to the rear of the train is the paddle steamer *Embassy.*

The useful little Adams B4 tanks were introduced in 1891 for dock shunting. No 30093 was withdrawn in April 1960 and the entire class was extinct by 1963; but two, No 30096 *(Normandy)* and No 30102 *(Granville),* have been preserved; the former on the Bluebell Railway and the latter at Bressingham Steam Museum. *6 August 1954.*

Swanage branch, Dorset *(right)*
Taken a couple of months before the engine was withdrawn, a pleasing study of M7 0-4-4T No 30060 as it bustles along between Corfe Castle and Wareham with the 15.38 (Sundays) working from Swanage.

The nine-mile branch on the Isle of Purbeck opened on 20 May 1885, a fairly late addition to the railway map. It connected Swanage, then with a population of just 2,000, with the main Southampton–Dorchester route at Worgret Junction; there was one intermediate stop at Corfe Castle. Although still well patronised in summer, the branch closed to passenger traffic on 3 January 1972; however, the section between Corfe Castle and Swanage has been rebuilt as the Swanage Railway and is now a highly popular tourist attraction.
7 May 1961.

Salisbury, Wiltshire (1)

A stirring sight: Southern Region's premier West Country train, the 'Atlantic Coast Express', hauled by Merchant Navy class No 35014 *Nederland Line,* prepares to stop at Salisbury, the cathedral city and important railway crossroads.

The eastern end of the station was a favourite place for trainspotters, who were used to the sight of heavy Waterloo-bound expresses struggling to retain adhesion on the sharp curve away from the platforms. This often resulted in spectacular and noisy bouts of slipping – particularly when a light-of-foot Bulleid Pacific was in charge! *29 September 1962.*

Salisbury, Wiltshire (2)

David and Goliath! The crew of Beattie 2-4-0WT No 30587 positioned their diminutive charge alongside the massive bulk of BR Class 9F 2-10-0 No 92231 outside Salisbury (72B) shed for Ivo Peters to record the appreciable contrast in size of these locomotives from different eras.

The now-preserved well-tank, of 1874 vintage, had worked for most of its life in

Cornwall on the Wenford Bridge branch and was captured during a brief sojourn at Salisbury on its way to Eastleigh Works, prior to withdrawal; it still carries the 72F shed plate of Wadebridge. No 92231, built in 1958, was also in temporary residence, being allocated to 71A Eastleigh depot; it was scrapped in April 1967. *29 September 1962.*

Salisbury, Wiltshire (3) *(above)*

A crowd of young trainspotters gathers at the west end of Salisbury station to watch the arrival of Battle of Britain class No 34056 *Croydon* with an express for Waterloo.

Visible over the locomotive is the GWR 93-lever Salisbury 'C' signal box, behind which are the lines to the GWR terminus, which closed on 12 September 1932. This dated from 30 June 1856, the opening of the broad-gauge line from Warminster. Beyond the SR's 64-lever 'B' signal box in the middle distance is Salisbury's busy motive power depot.

One of the batch constructed in 1947, No 34056 *Croydon* was rebuilt in December 1960. For many years it was based at 72A Exmouth Junction shed, before being transferred to 70E Salisbury in October 1963. It was eventually withdrawn in May 1967, spending three months in storage before being scrapped. *29 September 1962.*

Salisbury, Wiltshire (4) *(right)*

Get a grip! 70A Nine Elms Merchant Navy class No 35029 *Ellerman Lines*, with the down 'ACE', has trouble gaining adhesion on the slippery rails as it tries to re-start the heavy train, sending a towering column of black smoke into the heavens. On the footplate was Air Commodore C.M. Wight-Boycott, CBE, DSO, Commandant of the Royal Observer Corps, in which Ivo Peters was a chief observer until retirement in 1972.

The locomotive, which entered service in February 1949, was withdrawn in September 1966 having notched up some three-quarters of a million miles, the lowest recorded for any of the class. Having spent nearly seven years rusting in a scrapyard at Barry Docks, it was removed in January 1974 and is now preserved in a sectioned condition at the National Railway Museum, York. *28 October 1961.*

Wilton, Wiltshire

Under a leaden sky full of rain, the 12.00 (SO) Ilfracombe to Waterloo service, with rebuilt Merchant Navy Pacific No 35004 *Cunard White Star* in charge, passes through Wilton and heads towards Salisbury, 2¹/₂ miles distant.

The sidings on the left acted as a locomotive changing point for the much-vaunted 'Devon Belle' Pullman service to Ilfracombe and Plymouth, which ran for seven years between 1947 and 1954. The lack of water troughs on the Southern made this locomotive exchange necessary and avoided stopping for water at Salisbury, for the train was advertised as non-stop between Waterloo and Sidmouth Junction. *10 August 1963.*

Semley, Wiltshire
On the Southern main line near Semley, West Country class 4-6-2 34094 *Mortehoe* climbs the 1:100 bank through a deep cutting just west of the station with the 10.48 ex-Torrington portion of the 'Atlantic Coast Express', which was run in four parts on busy summer Saturdays. Semley's tall up home signal was a mixture of designs: the lattice post was of LSWR origins, whilst the upper quadrant arm was SR.

No 34094 was a 70A Nine Elms locomotive and remained in original condition throughout its service until withdrawn in August 1964 and, after being stored at 70D Eastleigh for a short period, was sent to Woodham's, Barry, where it was scrapped in November.
9 August 1958.

Buckhorn Weston Tunnel, Dorset *(left)*

With its demise in the offing, visits to the Southern's Exeter–Waterloo route were to become increasingly irresistible for Ivo Peters. He captured the last glorious decade of steam on this once-important main line before the Beeching era took its toll and it was downgraded to a single track. Set in a deep wooded cutting, the tunnel mouth, just west of Gillingham, provided the perfect setting to photograph the magnificent Bulleid Pacifics as they raced towards the capital with their 12-coach expresses.

On a sultry September day in 1961, rebuilt West Country class 4-6-2 No 34096 *Trevone*, working the 08.09 (SO) Torrington–Waterloo, pounds out of the 742yd tunnel on the 1:100 rising gradient and heads eastwards at speed towards London. *2 September 1961.*

Yeovil Town station, Somerset *(above)*

The station opened on 1 June 1861 and was jointly operated by the GWR and LSWR who left their individual marks on its design and signalling.

A shuttle service operated between Yeovil Town, Pen Mill station (on the GWR Weymouth line) and Yeovil Junction, about 1³/₄ miles to the south on the main Exeter–Waterloo route. This was usually the duty of an M7 tank, and here 0-4-4T No 30129 is viewed from Dodham Bridge with its two-coach push-pull train. Several other locomotives are seen on the right outside the busy shed. The station closed to passengers on 2 October 1966 and entirely on 9 October 1967; the shed remained open to house the Pen Mill-Junction DMU until the service was withdrawn from 6 May 1968. Sadly, today the whole station site forms the town's major open air car park. *5 August 1962.*

Lyme Regis branch, Dorset (1)
After a gestation period of over thirty years, the steeply-graded 6$\frac{1}{2}$-mile branch opened on 24 August 1903 – although it had been proposed in 1845. The tightly-curved line became noted as the stomping ground of the fabled ex-LSWR 4-4-2 Adams radial tanks of 1882 design that worked the branch from 1913 to 1960. Particularly suited to the task, the mainstays were Nos 30582 and 30584; but 30583 (erstwhile 488), which had worked on the East Kent Railway, joined them in 1946.

  This shot, taken on a bright spring morning, shows No 30584 with a train for Lyme Regis passing through a beautiful wooded section of the line near Bulmoor Cross.
18 April 1960.

Lyme Regis branch, Dorset (2)

With Ivo Peters' midnight blue Bentley Mk VI parked on the road opposite, Adams 4-4-2T No 30582 drifts under the bridge near Hook Farm, shortly after crossing Cannington Viaduct further round the bend in the background, and nears Lyme Regis with a train from Axminster. The branch closed on 29 November 1965, although it was turning in a small operating profit of five per cent.

Although Nos 30582 and 30584 were scrapped at Eastleigh Works in February 1962 and December 1961 respectively, No 30583 has been preserved on the Bluebell Railway in Sussex. *30 March 1959.*

Seaton Junction, Devon *(left)*
The road bridge at the eastern end of the station provided a superb view of trains as they passed through Seaton Junction, which was extensively rebuilt and widened in 1927–8 allowing two through lines to be laid, with loops to the extended platforms.

A busy scene indeed: Battle of Britain class No 34059 *Sir Archibald Sinclair* gets away with the 11.48 Plymouth–Waterloo, whilst a down local for Exeter waits opposite. A train on the Seaton branch, just visible behind the buildings on the extreme left, was probably a connecting service with the Waterloo-bound express. *18 July 1964.*

Honiton Tunnel, Devon (1) *(right)*
Some of Ivo Peters' best photographs were taken at the mouths of tunnels and this beautifully executed example is one. Rebuilt Bulleid Pacific No 35025 *Brocklebank Line* with the 08.25 Plymouth–Waterloo, rushes out of the 1,345yd tunnel into bright sunlight and down the 1:80 gradient through the deeply wooded cutting towards Seaton Junction 4¹/₂ miles away.

Despite its good condition, the locomotive, then based at 83D Exmouth Junction, was withdrawn from service just a month after this evocative picture was taken. No 35025 was eventually sent for scrap to Barry Docks in January 1965, but was spared the cutter's torch and currently awaits restoration on the Great Central Railway, Loughborough. *22 August 1964.*

Honiton Tunnel, Devon (2)

Taken on the same day as the previous picture, West Country class light Pacific No 34108 *Wincanton* bursts from the tunnel's western portal and drifts down the 1:90 grade with the 11.45 Waterloo–Ilfracombe. This end of the tunnel marked the summit of an almost continuous seven-mile climb, much of it at 1:80, including the testing Honiton Bank.

This was a popular location for the railway photographer: in steam days, the embankments were always kept beautifully trimmed and relatively clear of undergrowth; today it is an entirely different scene and nature has been allowed to run riot. *22 August 1964.*

GREAT WESTERN LINES

Hereford, Herefordshire
Resuming its journey southwards, No 1021 *County of Montgomery*, with the 10.30 (Sundays) Liverpool–Plymouth, carefully weaves out of Hereford station past Ayleston Hill signal box and approaches Ivo Peters' vantage point on the bridge to give him this bird's eye view of the Hawksworth-designed locomotive. The squat double-blastpipe chimney, with which the class was fitted in the late 1950s, is seen to good advantage; however, it did not improve the County's appearance.

Introduced in 1945, the County two-cylinder 4-6-0s produced a moderate performance, falling between a Castle and a Hall in terms of power and rated as 6MT. Relatively uninspiring in design, none of the class was preserved and No 1021 was scrapped by Hayes, Bridgend, in July 1964.
25 June 1961.

Charlbury troughs, Oxfordshire

Whilst in charge of an Oxford University Railway Society special, Castle class 4-6-0 No 5054 *Earl of Ducie* takes water from Charlbury troughs on the Oxford–Worcester line. Retaining much of its handsome appearance, No 5054 was one of the few of the class to keep its single chimney, although it was fitted with a less pleasing slab-sided Hawksworth tender.

The locomotive, then based at 85A Worcester shed, had only a few months left in service: it was withdrawn the following October and scrapped at Swindon Works during November. *16 May 1964.*

Fox's Wood troughs, Somerset

To enable traffic to run non-stop between Paddington and the West Country (and also to Newport via the Severn Tunnel), during the 1890s water troughs were installed on the main line at Goring in Berkshire and at Fox's Wood between Bristol and Keynsham. With the opening of the direct lines via Westbury and Badminton, these troughs were used less frequently and seldom needed.

Double-chimneyed Castle class 4-6-0 No 5057 *Earl Waldegrave* makes a splendid sight as it takes water at Fox's Wood whilst heading eastwards with the 13.50 Bristol–Paddington. *30 April 1960.*

Bristol Bath Road shed
A personal favourite: on one of his occasional visits to the two ex-GW sheds in the city, Ivo Peters took this glorious shot – which he captioned 'a study in chimneys'. It shows three distinctly different classes of GWR 4-6-0s standing outside Bath Road shed awaiting their next turn of duty. They are, from left to right: No 7033 *Hartlebury Castle*, No 6986 *Rydal Hall* and No 1009 *County of Carmarthen*.

The shed dated from 1933/4 and was built on the site of the old Bristol & Exeter Railway Works replacing an early structure and coaling stage. Bath Road shed (coded 82A) closed to steam in the autumn of 1960 and was completely rebuilt as a modern diesel depot. *16 August 1959.*

Winterbourne, Gloucestershire

Under the auspices of British Railways, in the 1950s Swindon carried out a series of tests, not only on their own locomotives, but on those from former rivals of the GWR, which had been rebuilt or modified in some way as an ongoing development of the steam locomotive.

    One such test involved an ex-LNER locomotive, Gresley V2 2-6-2 No 60845, which after being modified at Swindon was tried out on a 25-coach train from Reading to Stoke Gifford and back. After getting away faultlessly with its abnormally heavy load, it is seen on the return journey as it looms out of the fog, like a ghostly apparition, 1½ miles east of Stoke Gifford.
3 March 1953.

Twerton Tunnel, Somerset (1) *(left)*
The spectacle of a steam engine bursting out of a tunnel was always an attraction for the photographer. Having just emerged from the imposing turreted portal of Twerton Tunnel on the western outskirts of Bath and some two miles from the station, 4-6-0 No 4944 *Middleton Hall* makes a fine sight as it races towards the Georgian city with an express from Weymouth.

No 4944 was withdrawn from 81C Southall shed in September 1962 and subsequently scrapped by King's, Norwich, in January 1964. *30 April 1949.*

Twerton Tunnel, Somerset (2) *(above)*
Once more out of the breach, dear friends . . . perhaps! King class 4-6-0 No 6019 *King Henry V* dashes past Twerton Tunnel signal box with the 16.15 from Paddington to Plymouth. The signal box controlled two sidings, one either side of the line, but they were little used and by the 1960s had been lifted.

Introduced in 1927, the King class were the most powerful 4-6-0s built in Britain. Along with the Castle class, they were the mainstay of the GW/WR's crack expresses until the end of the summer service in 1962. *29 May 1950.*

Bath Spa, Somerset
(left)
Caught in the nick of time: Ivo Peters, standing on the up platform at Bath waiting to photograph the arrival of 4-6-0 No 6003 *King George IV,* just manages to click the shutter as 4-6-0 No 7036 *Taunton Castle* gets under way with an up express for Paddington. The King class locomotive was making a test run with a dynamometer car attached to the train to assess the practicability of improving the timings of the 'Bristolian'.
30 April 1954.

Sapperton Bank, Gloucestershire *(right)*
In sparkling condition shortly after emerging from a works overhaul, No 5990 *Dorford Hall,* with an up goods, makes an excellent unassisted climb of Sapperton Bank on the Gloucester–Swindon line at Brimscombe just south of Stroud. The summit of the climb, some of which was at 1:60, was reached inside Sapperton Tunnel before the line descended towards Kemble.
   From March 1960, No 5990 was based at 84C Banbury until it was withdrawn in January 1965, and scrapped on site by Friswells Ltd in June 1965.
   28 April 1962.

Upton Scudamore Bank, Wiltshire *(left)*
Although built by the Great Western, the line from Westbury to Salisbury became the operating responsibility of the Southern Region of BR from 2 April 1950. It diverged from the West of England main line at Westbury South Junction just south-east of the station and then climbed for over two miles – half of which was at 1:70 – to the summit at Upton Scudamore.

Power without the glory: BR Class 9F 2-10-0 No 92157, from 21A Saltley shed, climbs the bank lustily with a train of empty oil tanks for Fawley. A few months later this traffic was diverted from the route. *28 April 1962.*

Fairwood Junction, Wiltshire *(right)*
A mile from South Junction, where the Salisbury line diverged, Fairwood Junction marked the westerly connection with Westbury's avoiding line.

A stranger comes under the admiring gaze of the signal box's occupant. An impressive study of SR Merchant Navy class 4-6-2 No 35026 *Lamport & Holt Line* as it negotiates the junction after coming off the Westbury loop and heads westwards with a special working for Exeter. With the demise of BR steam getting ever closer, a number of specials ran over the West of England main line during the latter part of 1966. *15 October 1966.*

Norton Malreward, Somerset

The last days of steam on the old North Somerset line: Class 6100 2-6-2T No 6148 swings around the bend with the 17.00 goods from Radstock and nears Norton Malreward, just south of Whitchurch, with a load of coal for Portishead power station. The 2-6-2T was a regular performer on the line and based at 82B St Philip's Marsh shed, Bristol, until transferred to 83B Taunton a couple of months after this photograph was taken; it was withdrawn in September 1964.

The Bristol–Radstock section of the North Somerset line was scheduled to close on 30 June 1968, but it lingered on for a couple of weeks whilst signalling and track work was carried out on the Radstock–Frome section, to which traffic was to be diverted. In the event, a violent thunderstorm and torrential rain on 10 July caused serious slips at Pensford, precipitating its final closure four days early. *13 April 1964.*

Brewham, Somerset

On a warm summer's evening, ex-GWR 4-6-0 No 6945 *Glasfryn Hall* is seemingly framed by an arboreal umbrella as it makes a spirited climb of Brewham Bank, just nort-east of Bruton, with a Paddington–Weymouth train on the West of England main line.

No 6945 was allocated to 82F Weymouth shed, but ended its days working out of 88A Cardiff Canton MPD. It was withdrawn in September 1964 after many years of sterling service as a member of this versatile class of mixed traffic locomotive designed by Collett, introduced in 1928. *11 August 1956.*

Weymouth Harbour branch, Dorset *(left)*
A lovely study of Class 5700 0-6-0PT No 7780 as it threads its way at walking pace along Weymouth Quay with its goods train of vans. The mixed-gauge tramway came into use on 16 October 1865 for horse-drawn goods traffic (remaining so until about 1885), although the 'narrow' rails were not used until the end of broad gauge workings in 1874.

On 1 July 1889 boat trains started to use the tramway (then part of the Weymouth & Portland Railway and leased jointly by the GWR and LSWR) to connect with the Channel Island ferries. The GWR had been closely associated with the Weymouth & Channel Island Steam Packet Company since the town's station opened in 1857, but from 1876 they started to operate their own fleet of boats. For many years goods traffic was an important source of revenue for the railway, particularly fresh produce arriving at the port from the Channel Islands to be transported, as illustrated here.
7 May 1961.

Exeter St David's, Devon *(right)*
A brief respite: the normally busy St David's station seems remarkably quiet and railway staff enjoy a rest basking in the bright sun outside the shed on a warm spring afternoon, as 0-4-2T No 1434 stands over the ash pit adjacent to the coaling plant. Lurking in the background is Castle class 4-6-0 No 5075 *Wellington,* allocated to Exeter (83C) in July 1959; it was based at the shed for two years before being transferred to 87A Neath in August 1961. No 1434 had been at Exeter since January 1957, remaining so until withdrawal in July 1962.
24 April 1960.

MIDLAND LINES

Bath Green Park, Somerset

A famous visitor in the shape of Class 7P 4-6-0 No 46100 *Royal Scot*, with driver John Stamp at the controls, is seen leaving Bath Green Park with the up 'Pines Express', whilst Class 2P 4-4-0 No 40700, all but obscured by the drifting steam and smoke on this breezy day, stands on the shed road awaiting its next turn of duty on the S&D line.

No 46100, the doyen of the class and rebuilt in 1943 by Sir William Stanier from a 1927 Fowler design, was based at 16A Nottingham shed.
Withdrawn from BR service in October 1962, the locomotive was preserved and now resides at the Bressingham Steam Museum.
10 June 1961.

Bristol Barrow Road shed (1)
Sheds acted as a magnet for Ivo Peters and he took some memorable shots, including this one with which he was particularly pleased. The smoky gloom of Barrow Road's interior is dramatically illuminated by brilliant shafts of evening sunlight which are cast down on four different classes of locomotives seen at rest inside: 4F 0-6-0 No 44015, a 3F 0-6-0, a 'Jinty' 0-6-0T and a 'Black Five' 4-6-0. *17 February 1957.*

Bristol Barrow Road shed (2) *(left)*
A crowded scene: a variety of ex-Midland locomotives stand outside Barrow Road shed whilst a permanent way gang carries out repairs to one of the roads. In the foreground is a Class 3F 0-6-0, which has its chimney protected, suggesting it is in storage prior to withdrawal from service, or awaiting a repair at the works. On the immediate left is Class 2P 4-4-0 No 40426, which was withdrawn from service the following November and scrapped at Derby Works the same month. *17 February 1957.*

Bristol Barrow Road shed (3) *(right)*
Homeward bound: Patriot Class 6P 4-6-0 No 45504 *Royal Signals* coasts down past its motive power depot with the 07.00 Sheffield–Bristol service.
   The ex-Midland Railway shed (82E) was usually a hive of activity in steam days, as this dramatic shot taken from an adjacent building testifies. A variety of motive power is in residence: two Jubilee class 4-6-0s, a Stanier Class 5MT 'Black Five' 4-6-0, a Stanier 'Crab' 2-6-0 and two 'Horwich Crab' 2-6-0s, including No 42758. The large coaling plant is to be seen beyond the bridge in the background.
13 May 1961.

Wickwar, Gloucestershire (*above*)

Stanier Class 8F 2-8-0 No 48339, from Saltley (21A) shed, in charge of an up fitted freight, passes between two overbridges spanning a cutting on the approach to Wickwar Tunnel on the ex-Midland Bristol-Gloucester main line.

Introduced in 1935, the Class 8F 2-8-0s were another of Sir William Stanier's masterly designs. They were the workhorses of the LMR's long-distant freight workings, but occasionally utilised on passenger trains. In BR days all regions, except the Southern, had an allocation of these powerful machines. *13 May 1961.*

Lickey Incline, Worcestershire (*right*)

This notorious two-mile incline at 1:37^3/$_4$ virtually matched the steepest on any main line in the country. In the days of steam it was a severe test for any northbound train, which would invariably be banked from Bromsgrove to the summit at Blackwell. Until replaced in May 1956, for many years this was the province of the Midland Railway's fabled 0-10-0 No 2290 *Big Bertha*, built in 1919.

Here, following two miles of stout effort, Class 9F 2-10-0 No 92155, from 21A Saltley, breasts the summit at Blackwell with a northbound freight. *27 May 1961.*

Spondon, Derbyshire
On a vile day with rain teeming down to make the photographer's life difficult, ex-Crosti BR Class 9F 2-10-0 No 92026, from 16E Kirkby-in-Ashfield shed, passes the signal box at Spondon station with a freight on the Midland Region's Derby–Nottingham line.

The locomotive was transferred a number of times during its career, ending its days working out of 8H Birkenhead MPD, from where it was withdrawn from service in November 1967. *13 May 1964.*

Settle–Carlisle line

Arten Gill Viaduct, Yorkshire

Set remotely in rugged countryside, with East Baugh Fell rising in the background (the highest point of which is Knoutberry Haw standing at 2,204ft), the elegant sweeping structure of the 11-arch Arten Gill Viaduct provides the perfect setting for the lineside photographer to capture a memorable study.

Here BR Class 9F 2-10-0 No 92051 hauls a short up goods over the viaduct spanning Artengill Beck. The light coloured gable on the building in the middle distance is Dent station.

No 92051, from 12A Carlisle Kingmoor, was withdrawn some two months later; it was cut up by Motherwell Machinery Scrap Co, Wishaw, in February 1968. *8 August 1967.*

Dent station, Yorkshire

Set in splendid isolation and surrounded by spectacular scenery, at 1,150ft the station is the highest on any main line in England. Opened by the Midland Railway on 6 August 1877 it served a scattered rural community, but provided a vital lifeline during severe weather conditions. Dent closed on 4 May 1970, but was reopened on 14 July 1986 mainly for use by fellwalkers – although the buildings are now privately owned.

Here Class 8F 2-8-0 No 48517 with an up goods drifts through the station on the falling 1:264 gradient. Then based at 10D Lostock Hall, the locomotive was withdrawn from service two months after this photograph was taken. *10 August 1967.*

Mallerstang, Westmorland

Stanier Class 5 4-6-0 No 45227, in charge of a northbound freight, coasts downhill on Mallerstang Common and passes over the small four-arch viaduct (No 137) spanning Ais Gill, which flows into the River Eden in the valley below. The passage of the Settle & Carlisle line, cut along the fellside here, was nothing short of a remarkable feat of engineering and afforded splendid views to Mallerstang Edge on the other side of the valley.

Only after much persuasion by his great friend and fellow photographer, Derek Cross, did Ivo Peters visit the line, but then only on a few occasions towards the end of the days of steam. *12 June 1967.*

Ashby Magna, Leicestershire

Ivo Peters only visited the Great Central line, which had been under Midland Region control since 1958, on a few occasions when he was *en route* to photograph the ironstone lines in the Midlands. Here he captures Thompson B1 4-6-0 No 61186 as it prepares to stop at Ashby Magna station with a down local. The locomotive is carrying the 2F shed plate of Woodford, where it was stabled; it was withdrawn from service some eighteen months later and was scrapped at Darlington Works in January 1963.

This picture was taken shortly before construction commenced of the M1 motorway, which was to run parallel with the GC here.
4 June 1961.

Catesby Tunnel, Northamptonshire

At 3,000yd, Catesby was the longest tunnel on the Great Central's London extension and no fewer than 30 million bricks were used in its construction. With long radius curves and grades of no more than 1:176, the line allowed for fast running and was renowned for the speed of its loose-coupled mineral trains, which often exceeded 50mph, earning the soubriquet of 'runners' or 'windcutters'.

Here a typical Annesley–Woodford 'runner' with BR Class 9F 2-10-0 No 92013 in charge, bursts out of the tunnel's southern portal some three miles from its destination. The Annesley-based 9F was withdrawn in September 1966, but recently the Great Central Railway at Loughborough has collected together a train of mineral wagons such as these, to re-create the 'windcutters'. *7 October 1964.*

Culworth, Northamptonshire

Such was its grand scale, in both ambition and civil engineering, that the Great Central can only be described in superlatives. It was designed in the late nineteenth century by Sir Edward Watkin to connect his system of regional railways in the North with the continent via a Channel tunnel, but it eventually became a victim of the Beeching Axe and was closed on 3 September 1966.

This picture illustrates perfectly the attitude taken by Sir Edward Watkin and his fellow directors when planning the line: the spaciousness of the layout of this small country station is plain to see. Here WD Austerity 2-8-0 No 90299 passes Culworth with a coal train for Woodford.
4 June 1963.

Grayrigg loops, Westmorland (1)
This must be one of the most evocative shots taken in Westmorland by Ivo Peters. With storm clouds gathering over Fell Head, early morning sunlight catches rebuilt Patriot 4-6-0 No 45531 *Sir Frederick Harrison,* its nameplates already removed, pulling out of the up loop at Grayrigg on a humble freight duty, having waited for the passing of a Glasgow–Manchester express hauled by Britannia Class 7P 4-6-2 No 70039 *Sir Christopher Wren.*

The grubby external condition of the Patriot was perhaps indicative that it had not long to remain in service; in fact it was withdrawn only a month after this shot was taken. No 45531 was broken up at Campbell's, Airdrie, between January and March 1966. *15 October 1965.*

Grayrigg loops, Westmorland (2)

The overbridge at the south end of the loops was a favourite vantage point for Ivo Peters. Although his visits to the North-West were made too late to record the heyday of steam-hauled expresses over Shap, when the majestic Coronation class Pacifics ruled supreme, he nevertheless captured on film seemingly mundane scenes such as this, which are now equally lamented and irreplaceable.

The ever-changing weather moods on Fell Head provide a dramatic backcloth to Tebay-based Class 4 2-6-0 No 43035, bathed in sunlight, as it propels an engineers' train northwards, whilst, on the other line, the signals are off for an up express and Britannia class No 70025 *Western Star* waits in the up loop with a parcels train. *15 October 1965.*

Dillicar Common, Westmorland

This is arguably one of Ivo Peters finest shots taken in Westmorland and perhaps explains the enormous pleasure he derived from his visits to the region. With Carlin Gill separating the 1,747ft Uldale Head from the north-western slopes of Fell Head, along the foot of which the Roman-built Fairmile Road runs, an idyllic photographic setting is formed for the now-preserved Britannia class Pacific No 70013 *Oliver Cromwell,* seen in charge of an empty wagon train, as it trundles round the bend towards Lowgill at the southern end of Lune Gorge. *12 August 1967.*

The Lune Gorge, Westmorland

Perched on this hillside, Ivo Peters had a commanding view of trains as they passed through the magnificent gorge. With the River Lune running alongside the line at this point, there would be few locations which could surpass its beauty and tranquillity, which attracted him to it time and again; today the M6 has obliterated the bluff upon which he once stood.

With the fireman nonchalantly leaning from the cab taking a well-earned

breather, Stanier 'Black Five' 4-6-0 No 45394 heads southwards through the gorge with a train of spent ballast. At the bottom right of the picture is Ivo's friend, Norman Lockett, who photographs the train from the lineside. The fell in the middle distance is Jeffery's Mount, under which the Dillicar troughs are located, whilst the western slopes of Blease Fell are on the right.
21 September 1966.

Dillicar troughs, Tebay, Westmorland
On one of the few level stretches of the West Coast main line in the region, the water troughs just south of Tebay provided a replenishment point for locomotives on the ascent or descent of Shap.

How the mighty are fallen: a sad sight as a weary-looking Royal Scot class,

No 46160 *Queen Victoria's Rifleman*, now relegated to freight duties, passes over Dillicar troughs without topping up its water supply. The once-noble express locomotive, had not long to suffer this indignity, for it was withdrawn a month later and was scrapped by the Motherwell Machinery & Scrap Co, Wishaw, in July 1965. *21 April 1965.*

Shap Wells, Westmorland *(above)*
This was a favourite location for generations of railway photographers and Ivo Peters was no exception, naming this spot 'classic'. With the distant Howgills as a spectacular backdrop and the awesome ruggedness of the surrounding landscape, many memorable shots were obtained here, as trains tackled the gruelling climb of Shap.

No longer to be seen is the all-maroon express headed by a mighty Pacific pounding up the severe gradient towards the summit, only a humble freight working: on a breezy summer's day Stanier Class 5 4-6-0 No 45450, from 10D Lostock Hall, struggles unassisted with a bulk cement train on the arduous 1:75 four-mile section from Tebay. Despite its clean external condition, the locomotive was withdrawn three months later. *11 August 1967.*

Lune Viaduct, Westmorland/Yorkshire *(right)*
One of many specials worked in the mid-1960s by the celebrated Class A3 Pacific No 4472 *Flying Scotsman* was over the recently-defunct ex-LNWR Ingleton line. Here the train heads north over the impressive spans of Lune Viaduct near Sedbergh on the Yorkshire/Westmorland border. In the distance the imposing peak of Arant Haw, standing at 1,989ft above sea level, is shrouded in low cloud and mist on a typically dull autumn day.

The section from Lowgill to Ingleton had officially closed to regular traffic on 7 December 1964 and that from Ingleton to Clapham Junction on 1 March 1965, although passenger services – apart from main line diversions – had ceased on 1 February 1954. *4 September 1965.*

Ryhope, Sunderland, Co Durham (1)

The multiple track just south of Sunderland, running along the North Sea coast, was a busy section which provided ample opportunity to photograph a procession of coal trains as they plied between the area's collieries.

Often hampered by inclement weather during his visits to the region, here Ivo Peters captures ex-North Eastern Railway J27 0-6-0 No 65795 on a perfect summer's evening as it heads south with a train of empties for Silksworth Colliery. Then based at 52G Sunderland, the J27, one of a class first introduced in 1906, had only a month or so left in service before withdrawal; it was scrapped at Willoughby's, Choppington, in November 1967.
13 June 1967.

Ryhope, Sunderland, Co Durham (2)
A view looking in the opposite direction shows the multiple track on this section to better advantage. Although the landscape appears bleak with no trees in sight and only a few houses just visible in the distance, this picture has a certain magic about it and shows WD Austerity class 2-8-0 No 90382 in an environment which could also be fittingly summed up as 'austere', as it ambles along with a short coal train.

Then based at 52G Sunderland MPD, No 90382 had only three months left in service; it was finally scrapped at Hughes Bolckow Ltd, North Blyth, in October 1967. *13 June 1967.*

SCOTTISH LINES

Bridge of Allan, Stirlingshire

On ex-Caledonian Railway metals just north of Stirling, LMS Class 5 4-6-0 No 44674, complete with snowplough, is wreathed in smoke and steam as it plods north with a mixed freight for Perth. The locomotive was based at 12A Carlisle Kingmoor MPD, where, apart from a nine month spell in 1964 when allocated to 10D Lostock Hall, it remained until withdrawn from service in December 1967. *12 April 1963.*

Ayr, Ayrshire (1)

With a spectacular plume of exhaust creating a decidedly thick atmosphere, Stanier Class 5 4-6-0 No 45423 makes a spirited start from Ayr station with a relief for Glasgow. The Victorian grandeur of the Station Hotel in the background helps make this a memorable photograph, which Ivo Peters took on his only visit to the seaside town. This was the third station built at Ayr by the Glasgow & South Western, opened on 12 January 1886 and replacing the previous one 300yd due north. *18 October 1965.*

Ayr, Ayrshire (2)
Standing at the north end of the station, Ivo Peters manages to catch a 'crab'! With steam leaking from its cylinders, accentuated by a crisp autumn day without a cloud in the sky, 'Horwich Crab' 2-6-0 No 42861 with a train of coal empties is about to pass through the station as it heads southwards. The locomotive sports a 67C shed plate, which denotes it is from Ayr itself.
18 October 1965.

INDUSTRIAL LINES

Lambton Collieries Railway, Philadelphia, Co Durham
A large number of locomotives were used on the former Lambton Collieries Railway and the NCB motive power depot there provided a good source of photographic interest. A simple, but efficient, method of coaling engines was employed here: coal was discharged from hopper wagons standing on an overhead stage and down chutes into the bunkers of locomotives waiting below. Here 0-6-2T No 42, built by Robert Stephenson in 1920, is about to be coaled from rickety-looking wagons on the stage. Of note is the headgear of the Dorothea pit seen in the background on the extreme right.

Today the pit has been closed and none of the railway system exists other than some embankments, which in part are used as public walkways; in other areas they have been completely reclaimed. However, the locomotive sheds at the former Philadelphia Engine Works are used for storage. *13 June 1967.*

Littleton Colliery, Staffordshire
On a bright summer's day, 0-6-0ST *Robert Nelson No 4,* built by Hunslet in 1936 (maker's number 1800), arrives at Littleton Colliery with a train of empty wagons.
 Situated in the village of Huntington just north of Cannock, the colliery produced its first coal in 1902 and remained in production until midday on

10 December 1993, when it finally closed. It was subsequently demolished and only a winding wheel, placed at the former entrance to the site on the A34 trunk road, acts as Littleton's memorial.
6 June 1962.

Baddesley Colliery, Warwickshire
The colliery, in the No 4 area of the West Midland Division, was home to one of the most interesting locomotives owned by the NCB: built by Beyer, Peacock in 1937 (maker's number 6841), Garratt *William Francis* stands near the water tank in the company of a Giesl-fitted Austerity 0-6-0ST.

Located between Atherstone and Tamworth, the colliery had links to both the LNWR and Midland lines; however, the former was eventually severed, probably due to an awkward level crossing over the A5 trunk road. Baddesley Colliery closed in February 1989.
2 September 1965.

Kilmersdon Colliery, Somerset (left)

Having commenced production in 1878, this colliery near Radstock became one of the last two survivors in the once-large Somerset coalfield and was eventually closed in September 1973. Rail access to the pithead's system was gained via a self-acting incline spurred from the ex-GWR North Somerset Bristol–Frome line.

Built in 1929 by Peckett & Co of Bristol, this 0-4-0ST worked at the colliery until its closure and is seen here engaged in shunting duties. The weed-strewn tracks and a broken buffer on the locomotive lend a certain rustic charm to this now-vanished scene. However, the Peckett, now named *Kilmersdon,* has survived and resides on the West Somerset Railway at Washford. *29 April 1966.*

CEGB Hams Hall Generating Station, Warwickshire (above)

Located near Coleshill, this large coal-fired power station had an extensive railway complex to service it. With the massive cooling towers and lofty chimneys for an imposing background, two 0-6-0Ts, built by Robert Stephenson & Hawthorns (No 9 in 1944 and No 12 in 1955), take a rest from shunting duties whilst their picture is taken.

Whereas many photographers ignored the more mundane or less glamourous aspects of steam traction, Ivo Peters considered that industrial engines had a charm of their own. He would endeavour to spend at least a week of his annual holidays visiting industrial lines and locations like this. *3 October 1966.*

Pallion Shipyard, Sunderland, Co Durham *(left)*
William Doxford & Son Ltd used several unusual crane-tanks besides more orthodox locomotives within their shipyard complex in Sunderland. Seen at rest outside their shed at the end of a day's work are, from left to right, *Hendon* (1940), *Southwick* (1942) and *Millfield* (1942), all built by Robert Stephenson & Hawthorns; *Pallion,* built by Hawthorn Leslie in 1902, and *General,* built by Peckett in 1944. *13 June 1967.*

Longmoor Military Railway, Hampshire *(right)*
An evocative study of the now-preserved Army Department 2-10-0 No 600 *Gordon,* in charge of an RCTS special on the Longmoor Military Railway near Liphook. The immaculately-kept locomotive hauled the train for part of both the outwards and return journeys. Today No 600 *Gordon* resides on the Severn Valley Railway. *30 April 1966.*

NARROW-GAUGE LINES

Isle of Man Railway (1)

With an abundance of pure-white steam issuing from their exhausts, two Beyer Peacock 2-4-0T locomotives, No 12 *Hutchinson* banked in the rear by No 13 *Kissack,* leave the Douglas terminus with the 10.20 for Port Erin. No 12 was built in 1908, whilst No 13 dated from 1910.

Ivo Peters visited the Isle of Man a number of times to photograph and film this delightful 3ft-gauge railway. At first he had met with some resistance from the private railway's general manager but, following a fortuitous meeting over a glass of ale in the station bar, this objection was soon overcome! *27 June 1961.*

Isle of Man Railway (2)

'I must down to the seas again, to the lonely sea and the sky . . .'. A light engine, believed to be Beyer Peacock 2-4-0T No 11 *Maitland* (maker's number 4663) of 1905 vintage, presents an enchanting sight as it saunters northwards along the scenic coastal section of the railway about mid-point between St John's and Kirk Michael. St Patrick's Isle and the town of Peel, to which a branch line from St John's ran, can just be seen in the distance and on the hillside above stands Corrin's Folly. *27 June 1961.*

Isle of Man Railway (3)

With the summer's sun high in the heavens, this is a superb study of 2-4-0T No 8 *Fenella* (built by Beyer Peacock in 1894), viewed from the A4 road as it crosses Glen Mooar Viaduct, working the 13.45 from Ramsey. There were two notable viaducts on the line a mile or so apart, the other being Glen Wyllin near Kirk Michael. In spite of its tourist potential and delightful appeal, the three-coach train would appear to have only a half-dozen or so passengers to relish the wonderfully scenic trip along the western side of the island as it headed towards Douglas via Kirk Michael and St John's.

The same journey cannot be made today following the final closure of this part of the railway in September 1968, despite several valiant attempts to save it. *27 June 1961.*

Welshpool & Llanfair Railway, Montgomeryshire

A quintessentially Welsh narrow-gauge scene: this 2ft 6in line runs through some of the most beautiful countryside in the principality, as this picture testifies. Cows look on with curiosity as a short goods train passes by, crammed with members of the Locomotive Club of Great Britain, who organised this special excursion. Hauled by 0-6-0T No 822 *The Earl* (built by Beyer Peacock in 1902), the train, complete with a cock-eyed LCGB headboard, is photographed by Ivo Peters, who followed it by car and took this picture about a mile out of Welshpool. The light railway is still operating today: each year some twenty-three thousand visitors flock to see it – and *The Earl,* together with other preserved locomotives. *23 June 1956.*

Dinorwic Quarries, Llanberis, Caernarvonshire (1)

The extensive slate quarries at Llanberis were served by a 1ft 10³/₄ in-gauge system and several 0-4-0 saddle tanks were employed. Here *Dolbadarn,* built by Hunslet in 1922, is seen emerging from a short tunnel hewn through the slate formation within the quarry complex.

The slate quarries of North Wales were a strong magnet for Ivo Peters, as they teemed with diminutive locomotives like this quaint example, which was basic in the extreme and offered the driver no protection from the elements. Many were considerably older than *Dolbadarn* and dated from the latter part of the nineteenth century. *27 September 1961.*

Dinorwic Quarries, Llanberis, Caernarvonshire (2)

From an elevated position within the quarry, Ivo Peters obtains an excellent view which provides a perfect impression of Dinorwic's railway system with its interlaced lines winding through the complex. Here, the ancient tank locomotive *Cackler*, built by the Hunslet Engine Co Ltd in 1898, hauls a set of empty wagons towards the buildings which have neat rows of trimmed slate stacked outside.

Today the historic Dinorwic Quarry workshops and part of the railway system form a museum for the largely defunct slate industry and operate under the auspices of the National Museum of Wales. *26 June 1956.*

Dinorwic Quarries - Padarn Railway, Caernarvonshire
'The western wind was wild and dank with foam, And all alone went she . . .'.
Hunslet 0-6-0T *Amalthea,* built in 1886, seen running back light engine on the 4ft-gauge 'main line' to Port Dinorwic, passes the shores of Llyn Padarn on a stormy autumn day, with the mountains of Snowdonia looming menacingly in the background.

Today a two-mile section of the line (rebuilt to 1ft 11½in gauge) is preserved and run under the auspices of the Llanberis Lake Railway. *27 September 1961.*

Penrhyn Railway, Caernarvonshire (1)

The 6^1/$_2$-mile, 1ft 11^3/$_4$in-gauge line linked the slate quarries at Bethesda with Port Penrhyn. Three 0-4-0 saddle-tanks, built by the Hunslet Engine Co Ltd, worked the 'main line', whilst somewhat smaller locomotives were employed in the actual quarries. With deep pine woods to its right, the immaculate 0-4-0ST *Blanche,* of 1893 vintage, complete with bucket hanging on the smokebox door containing sand to improve grip on slippery rails, approaches Felin-hên with a set of empty wagons.

Blanche's twin, also built in 1893, was named *Linda,* whilst the third, *Charles,* was constructed eleven years before. Although the railway closed in 1965, the three locomotives have survived: the 'girls', now considerably modified, run on the Festiniog Railway and *Charles* resides at Penrhyn Castle Museum. *27 June 1956.*

Penrhyn Railway, Caernarvonshire (2)
So enchanted was he by the narrow-gauge lines, particularly those serving the slate quarries, Ivo Peters made regular pilgrimages to North Wales to photograph the host of delightful little locomotives still employed (the last to be seen working in the quarries was *Winifred* in May 1965).

Framed to perfection: with an elegant iron bridge spanning the bubbling mouth of the Afon Cegin in the foreground, 0-4-0ST *Linda* arrives back at Port Penrhyn with a train of slate from the quarries. *27 September 1961.*

Talyllyn Railway, Merioneth

A sunny morning scene at Towyn (Tywyn): 0-4-0WT No 6 *Douglas*, built by Andrew Barclay in 1918 (maker's number 1431), is about to leave Wharf Station for Abergynolwyn with a train packed full of excited holidaymakers.

The first railway to be preserved, over forty years ago, the picturesque 7¼-mile line of 2ft 3in gauge still attracts many thousands of visitors each year and *Douglas* is a regular performer in traffic. *3 June 1963.*

Kettering Quarries, Northamptonshire
Ironstone used to be extracted extensively in the Midlands and many quarries had their own railway system, four of which were narrow gauge and worked by steam locomotives; Kettering Quarries' railway was of 3ft gauge.

Judging by its towering plume of exhaust, 0-6-0 saddle tank *Kettering Furnaces No 8* (Manning Wardle No 1675 of 1906) makes a stout effort as it passes through the fields with a heavy load of iron ore. *13 May 1960.*

Isle of Purbeck, Dorset
The delightful private light railway of Pike Brothers, Fayle & Co Ltd of Wareham, on the unique gauge of 2ft 8in, ran from the company's clay mines near Creech to the SR line at Furzebrook. No fewer than five locomotives were employed by the company: *Tertius* (rebuilt by makers Manning Wardle of Leeds, 1911), *Quintus* (Manning Wardle, No 1854 of 1914), *Sextus* (Peckett, Bristol, No 1692 of 1925), *Septimus* (Peckett, No 1808 of 1930) and 0-6-0WT *Secundus* (Bellis & Seekings, 1894).

Passing through a sunlit glade deep in the woods, *Quintus*, with a train of clay wagons, offers a spectacle to the photographer which today would seem almost unbelievable as a working industrial railway set in such an agreeable environment. *11 August 1954.*

Bicton Woodlands Railway, Devon

This charming 1ft 6in-gauge line runs through the grounds of Bicton Gardens near East Budleigh. Surrounded by towering pine trees, which seem to dwarf it, the immaculately-kept Avonside 0-4-0T *Woolwich,* of 1916 vintage, is seen returning through the woods with its train filled to capacity with visitors.

The lady seen to the immediate left of the locomotive is Angela O'Shea, Ivo Peters' housekeeper, who has just captured the passing train on colour film with her own camera. Bicton Gardens and the little railway are still very popular today and attract a large number of visitors each year. *26 June 1966.*

Kenmare, Co Kerry

Spending several summer holidays in the south-west of Ireland between 1948 and 1951, Ivo Peters made sure he included Kenmare on his itinerary. The station was the terminus of the former Great Southern & Western's branch from Headford Junction. In the summer of 1951 there were two trains a day, often of ancient mixed stock – some of it very quaint!

This splendid shot illustrates the point well: Class D19 No 13, designed by Alexander MacDonnell for the GS&W and built in 1877 (rebuilt at Inchicore Works in 1900), stands at Kenmare with the 13.15 mixed train for Headford Junction. Opened on 4 October 1893, Kenmare station closed on 1 January 1960, whilst Headford Junction remained open until 9 September 1963. *30 June 1951.*

Tralee & Dingle Light Railway, Co Kerry (1)

From Tralee in County Kerry, this delightful 3ft-gauge line ran for 31 miles to Dingle through the rugged splendour of the Dingle peninsula. It was hopelessly uneconomic and from 1947 only one train a month, a cattle special, ran to serve Dingle Fair. The line climbed to 684ft above sea level to cross the Slieve Mish mountain range and the gradients were very severe, much of it at 1:30, and trains averaged little more than 10mph.

A typical encounter at Tralee: sheep are driven past Hunslet 2-6-0 No 8T (built in 1910) with its eccentrically composed train of mixed stock. The footplate crew look on with amusement – probably because somebody was actually bothering to photograph this 'ordinary' scene! From the terminus of the narrow-gauge T&D, a line ran through the streets of Tralee to some exchange sidings in the standard-gauge goods yard nearby. *5 July 1950.*

Tralee & Dingle Light Railway, Co Kerry (2)

On a glorious sunny Friday in June 1951, Ivo Peters followed a cattle train for its entire journey between Tralee and Dingle, which took 3³/₄ hours, taking some memorable photographs *en route,* of which these are a small selection.

The train, hauled by Hunslet-built 2-6-0s No 1T and No 2T of 1889 vintage, climbed for four miles to Glenmore Pass, reaching the summit at Glenagalt Bridge and is seen here, having almost completed its traverse of the Slieve Mish mountains, crossing the main road near Emalough where there was once a station. It had closed on 17 April 1939, the day passenger services on the T&D were withdrawn. *29 June 1951.*

Tralee & Dingle Light Railway, Co Kerry (3)
The westbound cattle train crosses the impressive Lispole Viaduct with the mountains providing a spectacular backdrop to a scene which, in another two years, would become just a memory; the line finally closed in 1953. Lispole once had a station, which opened on 31 March 1891, but was closed on 17 April 1939. *29 June 1951.*

Tralee & Dingle Light Railway, Co Kerry (4)

With the mountains in the background, including the peak of Croagskeard at 2,001ft, No 1T and No 2T still have a certain amount of hard climbing to do as the train nears Dingle and runs alongside the main road to the town.

This marvellous scene from another age will never be replicated, but Ivo Peters has left these unforgettable images as a legacy of this wonderfully individual narrow-gauge railway on the Dingle peninsula; however, a section of the line between Tralee and Blennerville has been reopened, with trains hauled by No 5T, another Hunslett 2-6-0. *29 June 1951.*

INDEX OF PHOTOGRAPHS

NOTE: The county names given in the headings are those at the time when the photographs were taken and before the 1974 changes.